How They Make Bikes?

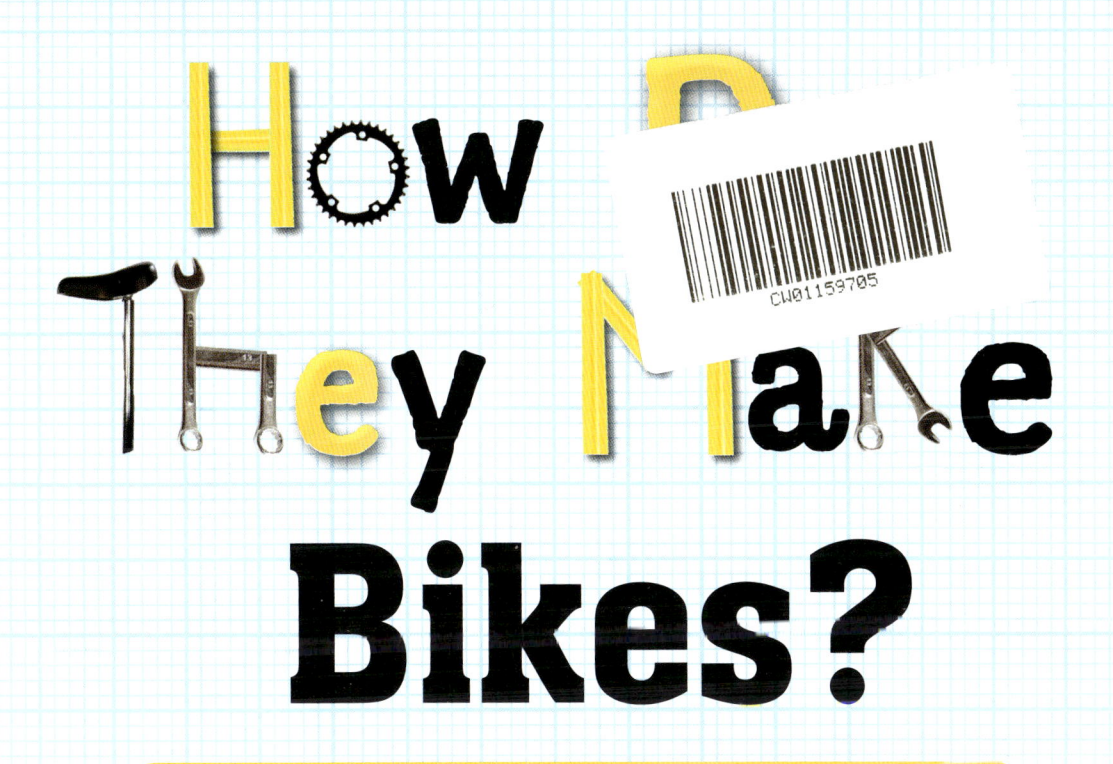

Contents

Cycling past	2
In the design studio	4
Making the frame	6
Any colour you like	8
On two wheels	10
Tyres and treads	12
Pedal power	14
Going fast and slow	16
In the saddle	18
Putting it all together	20
Sports and races	22
To the bike shop	24
Bits and pieces	26
Safety first	28
Looking after your bike	30
Glossary and index	32

Written by Neil Morris   Illustrated by Anthony Rule

Cycling past

The first bikes

The first bike was made nearly 200 years ago. It was called a dandy-horse, and it was very different from a modern bike. It was made of wood and it had no pedals.

The dandy-horse had no brakes. You pushed the ground with your feet to make it go.

The word *bike* is short for *bicycle*, which means 'two wheels'. Some early bikes had two very different wheels. The wheel at the front was gigantic, but the wheel at the back was tiny. This bike was called a penny-farthing, and it was difficult to ride!

Think about it!

In the 19th century, a penny was a large coin, and a farthing was a very small coin. Can you guess why the bike was called a penny-farthing?

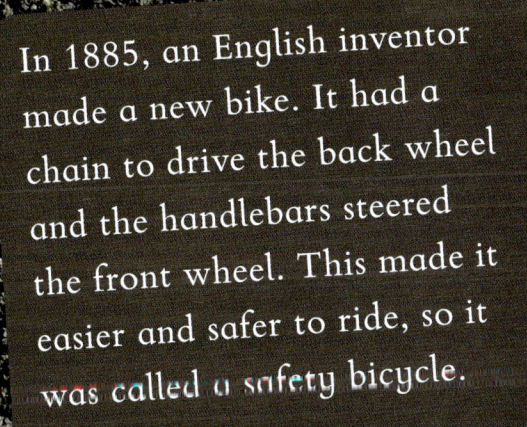

In 1885, an English inventor made a new bike. It had a chain to drive the back wheel and the handlebars steered the front wheel. This made it easier and safer to ride, so it was called a safety bicycle.

Most modern mountain bikes are similar to the old safety bicycle.

DID YOU KNOW?

- In 1895, more than 800 000 bikes were made in Britain.
- By 1900, about 4 million Americans were riding bikes!

IN THE DESIGN STUDIO

WHO MADE YOUR BIKE?

About 120 million bikes are made every year! China is the biggest producer of bikes, and India is the second biggest producer. Lots of different people take part at different stages of the production process, but it all starts with a designer.

DID YOU KNOW?
There are more than a thousand million (1 000 000 000) bikes in the world. End-to-end they would stretch to the Moon and back — twice!

A designer has to work out measurements and materials for the new bike.

MY JOB

Bike designer

"I work in a **design studio**, and it's my job to think up new designs for bikes and find ways to make bikes work better. I start by making **sketches** on paper. Then I use a computer to draw the bike in more detail. I check my design before **engineers** make the first model of my bike. We try the model out to make sure it all works properly before more bikes are made in a factory."

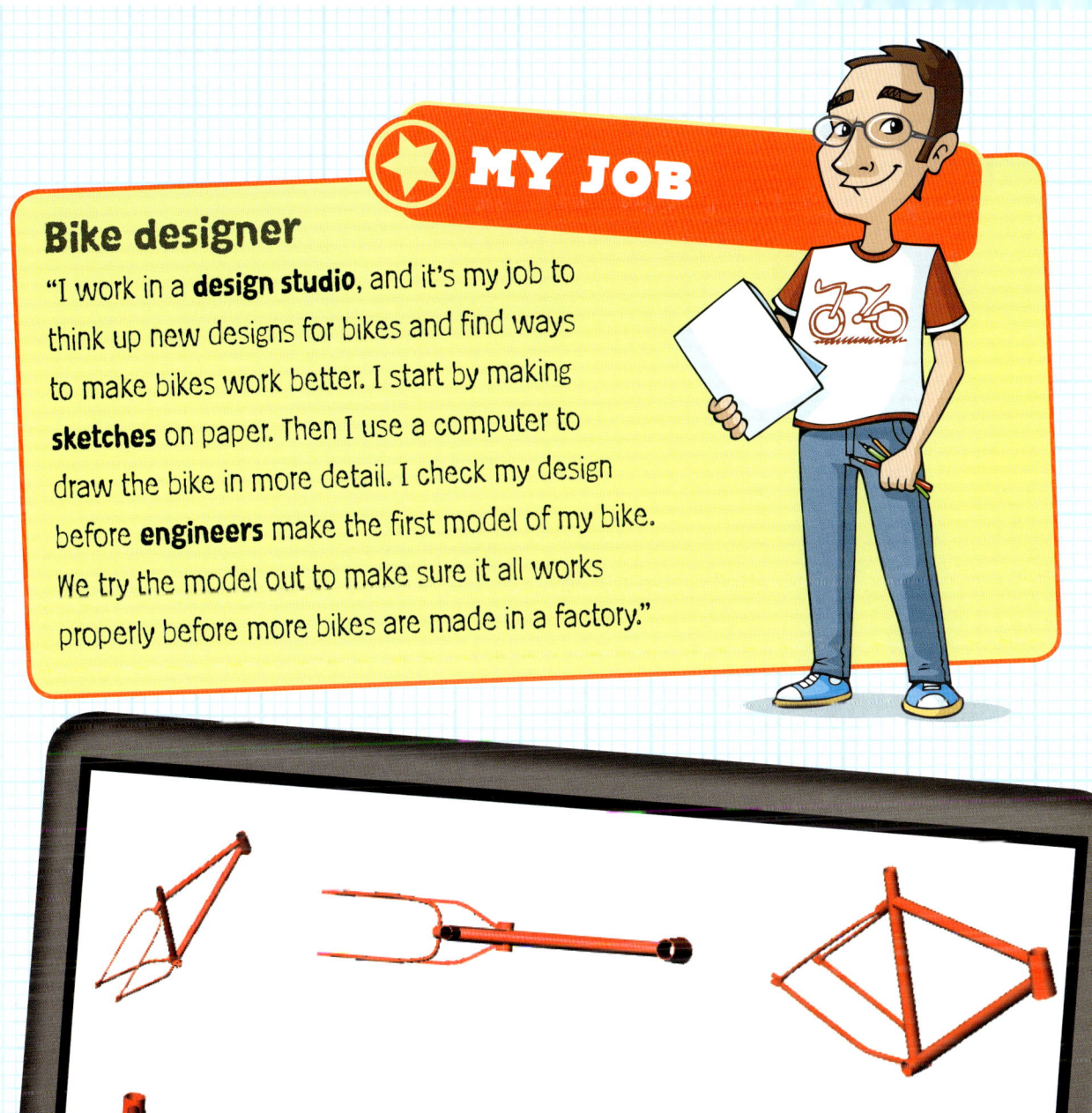

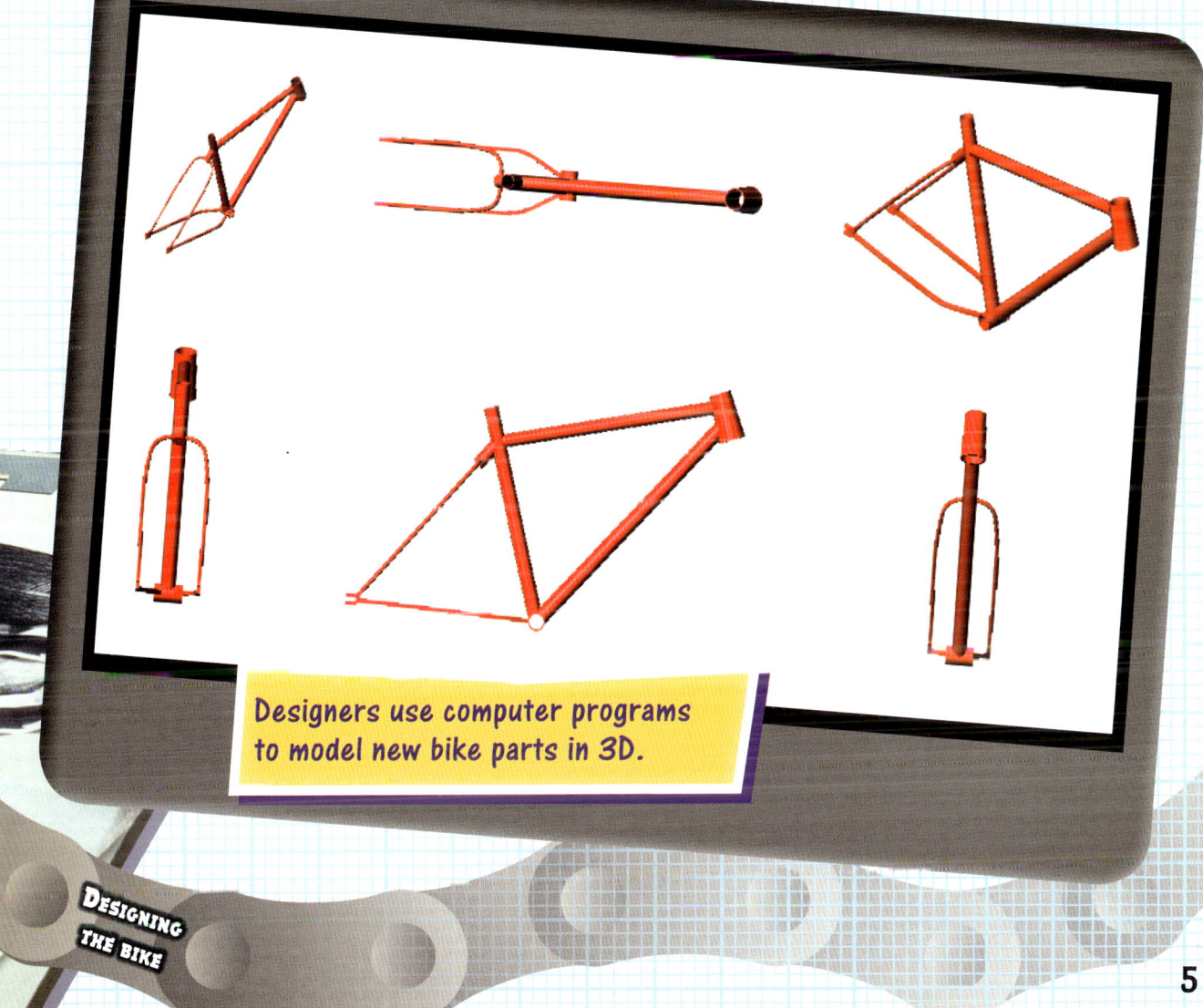

Designers use computer programs to model new bike parts in 3D.

DESIGNING THE BIKE

MAKING THE FRAME

SQUEEZING OUT TUBES

The main part of a bike is called the frame. It is made of strong metal tubes so that it can hold the rider's weight. The metal is usually steel, the same as most food cans, but on a frame it's much thicker. To make the tubes, hot steel is **extruded**. This means the metal is heated up and forced through a ring-shaped opening by a strong tool. It's a bit like squeezing out toothpaste! The frame tubes are then **welded** together. This makes a single, strong frame.

Welders wear special helmets to protect them from the bright light, strong heat and sparks.

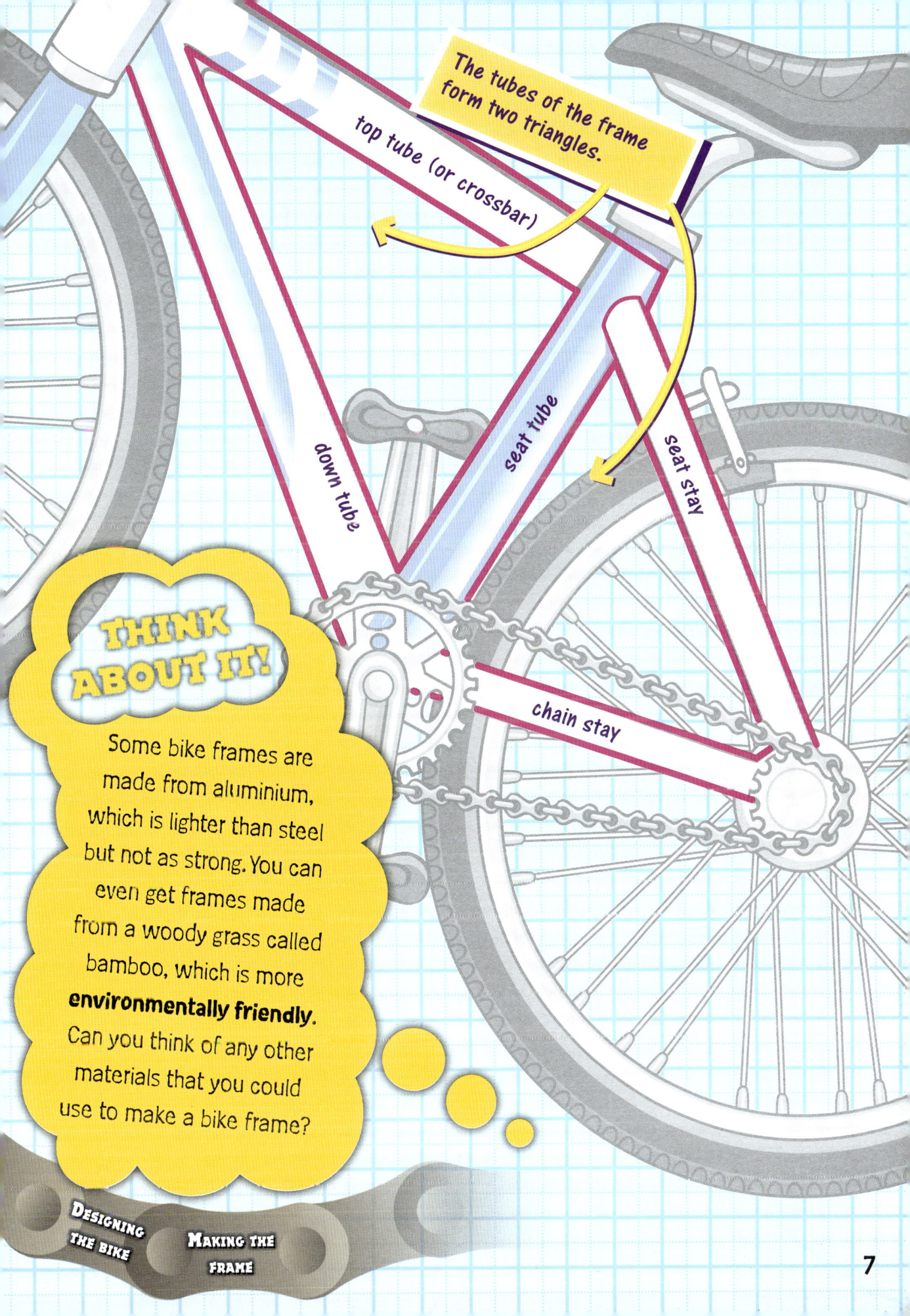

The tubes of the frame form two triangles.

top tube (or crossbar)

down tube

seat tube

seat stay

chain stay

THINK ABOUT IT!

Some bike frames are made from aluminium, which is lighter than steel but not as strong. You can even get frames made from a woody grass called bamboo, which is more **environmentally friendly**. Can you think of any other materials that you could use to make a bike frame?

DESIGNING THE BIKE | MAKING THE FRAME

Any colour you like

Spray and sticker

Steel and aluminium are grey. Bikes would look very boring if they were all the same dull grey, so colour is added to the frame. In a large bicycle factory, the frames pass through a spray room. The sprays give the bike frame an even coat of colour.

In smaller factories, workers spray the paint on by hand, and they can apply several colours to different parts of the frame. Once all the paint is dry, the workers add transfers and stickers. Some of these show the make and model of the bike: for example, the model name might be *Red Racer* or *Super Sport*.

The frames are hung up for spraying, so that every bit can be coloured.

On some bikes, the special effects are on more than just the frame.

SPECIAL EFFECTS

Some workshops use paints and transfers to create special effects, such as a snake-skin or a leopard-skin look. They can make a bike look as though it's made of wood, or they can give it a glossy, space-age effect. The possibilities are endless!

Try It!
Can you think up a model name for a bike? Design a logo and a sticker to put on your bike.

DESIGNING THE BIKE • MAKING THE FRAME • PAINTING THE FRAME

ON TWO WHEELS

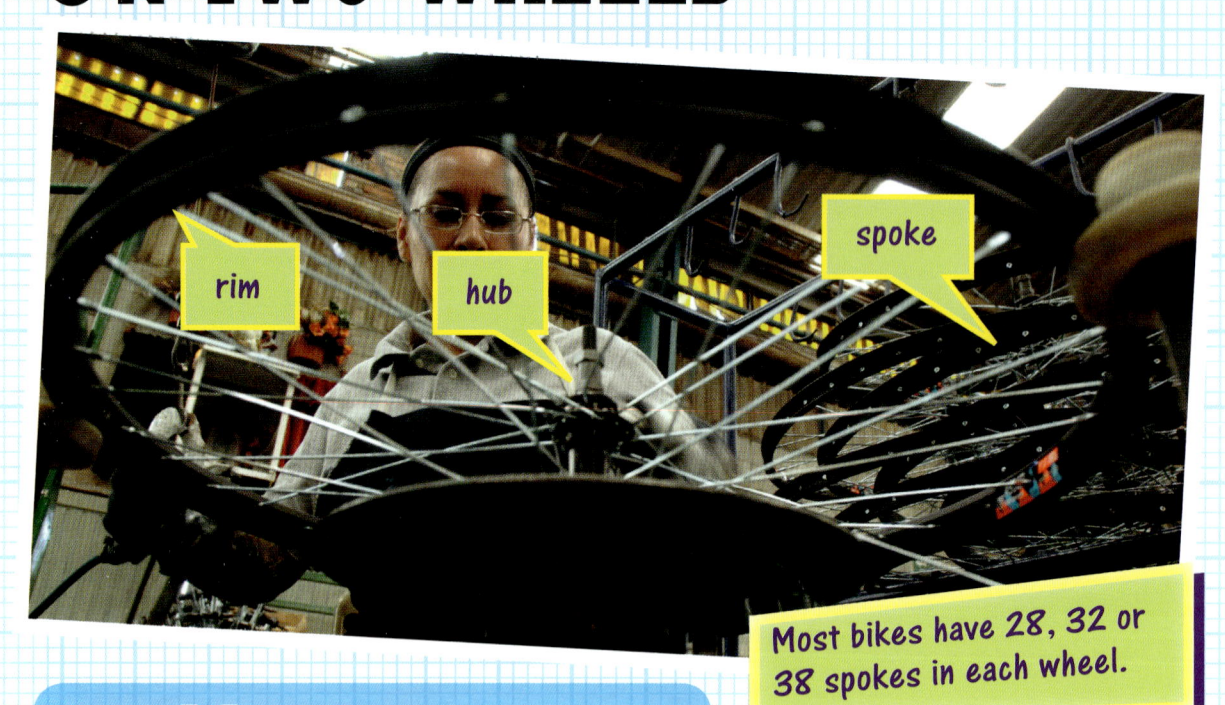

rim hub spoke

Most bikes have 28, 32 or 38 spokes in each wheel.

PUTTING A WHEEL TOGETHER

A bike's wheels are usually made from aluminium or steel. Each one has a round part, called a rim, for the tyres to sit on. The rims are made in a similar way to the frame – a long line of metal is squeezed into a shape and then bent into a circle. The rim is then connected by lots of thin steel spokes to a hub, which forms the middle of the wheel.

MY JOB

Wheel-builder

"I work in a factory that makes wheels for bikes. I use a special machine to connect all the parts of the wheel. Then I check that all the spokes are tight and that the wheel is perfectly round. The spokes can bend slightly if the wheel hits a bump, but they keep the wheel strong."

GETTING BIGGER

It's much easier and safer to ride a bike that is the right size for you.

Shops sell junior bikes by the size of their wheels. They measure across the middle of the wheel. This is just a rough guide, as the size that's right for you will depend on how tall you are.

Age	Wheel size
6 – 8 years	18 inches (46 cm)
7 – 9 years	20 inches (51 cm)
8 – 11 years	24 inches (61 cm)
11 and older	26 inches (66 cm)

Designing the bike · Making the frame · Painting the frame · Making the wheels

Tyres and Treads

Getting a Grip

Tyres are made in a different factory to the metal parts of the bike. In the past, they were made of natural rubber, which comes from the juice of rubber trees. Today factories use **synthetic** rubber, which is a squashy kind of plastic made from oil.

The rubber is laid onto a layer of **nylon** cloth to make the side of the tyre. The rubber is then heated up and pushed into a **mould**, which makes the tread pattern. The tread gives the tyres grip and stops them from skidding when you ride your bike.

DID YOU KNOW?

The Scottish inventor, John Boyd Dunlop, made the first blow-up tyres in 1887. They were for his son's tricycle – a bike with three wheels!

If you are cycling over rough ground, you need deeper treads than for cycling on roads.

Before each tyre is put on a wheel, a thin rubber tube is added. This is called an inner tube, and it sits between the tyre and the rim. It is filled with air to make the tyres firm and to give you a comfortable ride.

Try It!

Take the cap off the valve on your tyre. Screw the pump nozzle onto the **valve**, then pull the pump handle up and push it down again. Every time you push, you'll force air into the inner tube and make the tyre harder.

valve

pump nozzle

Designing the bike   Making the frame   Painting the frame   Making the wheels   Making tyres

13

Pedal power

ALL LINKED UP

Bike pedals are made from moulded plastic, aluminium or steel and they are connected to the cranks, which are fixed to a chain ring. A chain ring is a metal wheel with teeth. Its teeth fit into the bike's chain, which is connected to a **cassette** on the bike's back wheel.

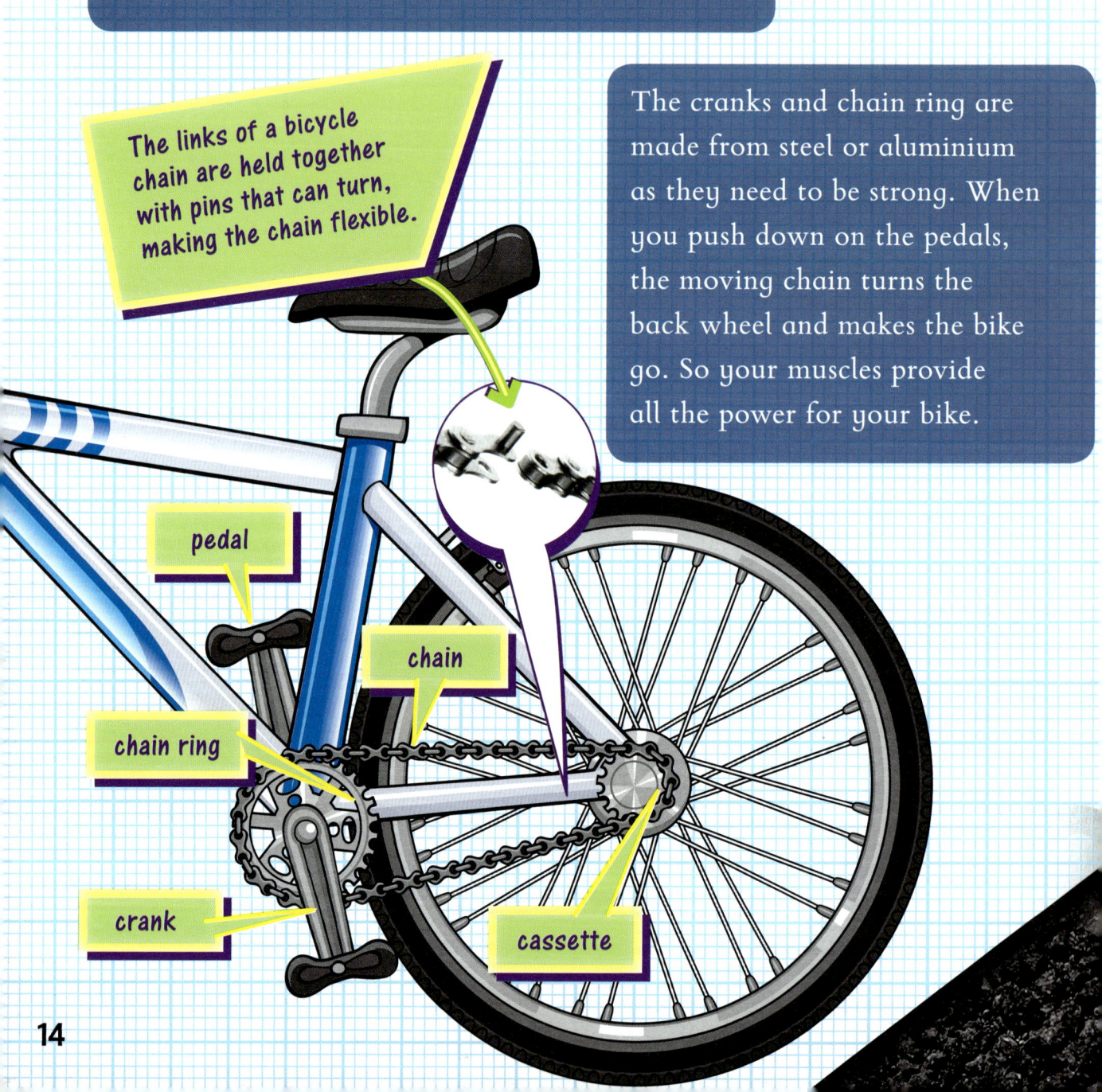

The links of a bicycle chain are held together with pins that can turn, making the chain flexible.

The cranks and chain ring are made from steel or aluminium as they need to be strong. When you push down on the pedals, the moving chain turns the back wheel and makes the bike go. So your muscles provide all the power for your bike.

- pedal
- chain
- chain ring
- crank
- cassette

Riders have to work together on a tandem, leaning the same way and pedalling at the same time.

DID YOU KNOW?
A tandem has two wheels, two sets of pedals and two seats. It is a bike for two riders!

Designing the bike Making the frame Painting the frame Making the wheels Making tyres Pedals and chain

15

Going Fast and Slow

Gearing Up and Down

Gears make pedalling easier. There are low and high gears, which the rider chooses with a shifter on the handlebars. The gear shifter is moulded from plastic, and it works a steel cable inside a plastic tube, which moves the gears back and forth.

In a low gear, the bike moves a short distance for every turn of the pedals. This makes it easier to ride uphill at a slow speed. High gears make the bike travel further for every turn of the pedals, which is useful for going downhill at a faster speed.

A bike with lots of gears has a cassette of different sprockets for the chain to slip on to.

A good rider changes gear whenever they go up or down a hill.

Designing the bike · Making the frame · Painting the frame · Making the wheels · Making tyres · Pedals and chain

16

THINK ABOUT IT!

Why do some bikes have lots of gears and others have none? Top-of-the-range racing bikes have up to 30 gears so they can race up and down hills more quickly. Other bikes have no gears, which makes them easy to ride on flat ground. How many gears does your bike have?

STEERING AND STOPPING

Handlebars are made in the same way as the frame tubes and are then bent into shape. Rubber grips are added to make them comfortable to hold. Two moulded plastic or steel levers are fixed to the handlebars to work the brakes, which are pieces of hard rubber that push against the wheels to slow and stop the bike.

rubber brake pads

Most handlebars are made of aluminium or steel.

Gears and brakes

IN THE SADDLE

A SEAT IN LAYERS

Most saddles are made from different kinds of plastic. The main part is a base of hard plastic, which is shaped in a metal mould. Then plastic foam is glued onto the base to make it softer. Finally a fabric cover is stretched over the saddle. A metal frame is attached underneath with bolts, so that the saddle can be fixed to the seat post of the bike.

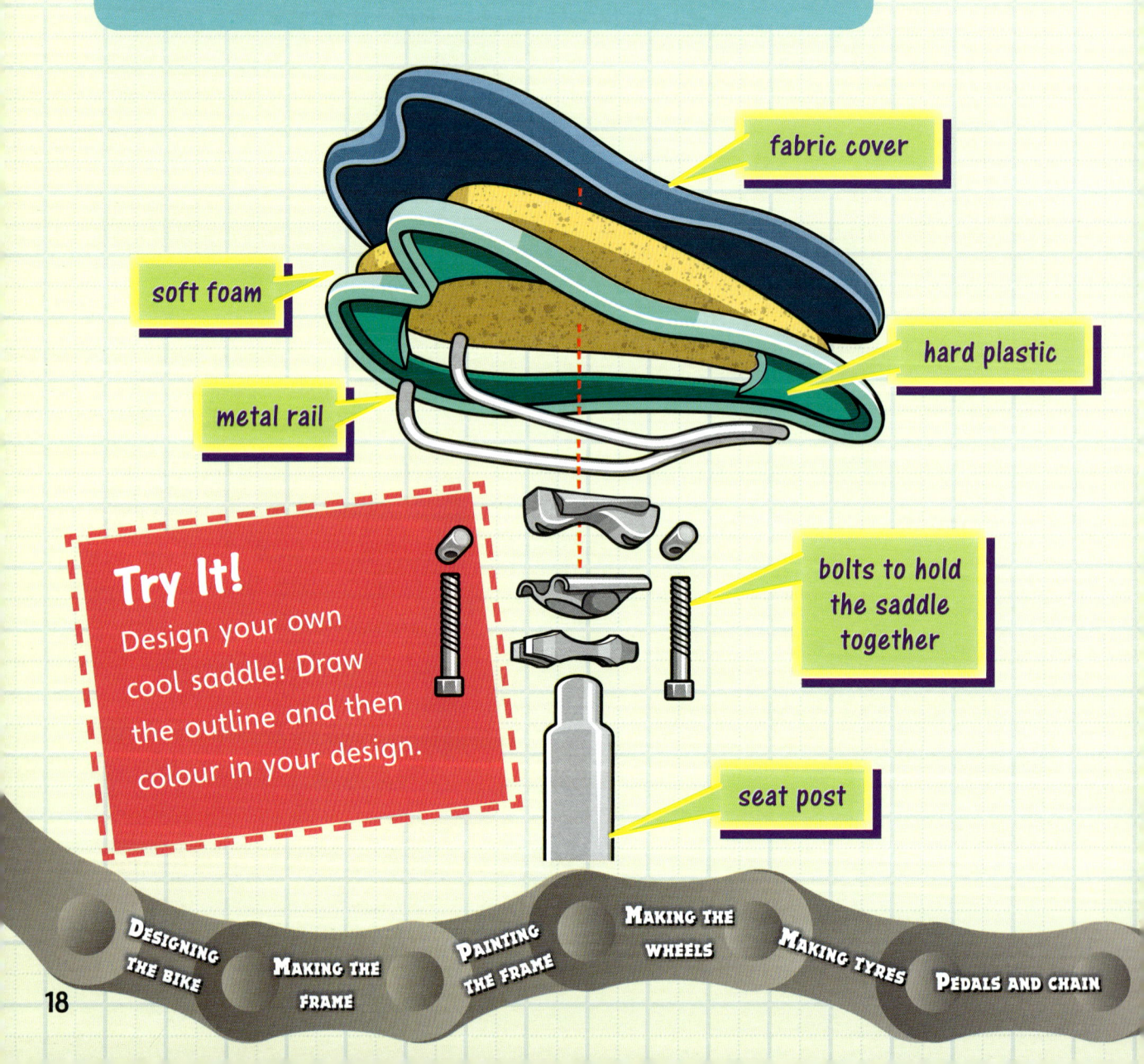

fabric cover

soft foam

hard plastic

metal rail

bolts to hold the saddle together

seat post

Try It!

Design your own cool saddle! Draw the outline and then colour in your design.

DESIGNING THE BIKE · MAKING THE FRAME · PAINTING THE FRAME · MAKING THE WHEELS · MAKING TYRES · PEDALS AND CHAIN

SITTING COMFORTABLY

John Brooks sold horse-riding saddles in Birmingham, England. When his horse died, in 1878, Brooks borrowed a friend's bicycle. He found the wooden seat uncomfortable, so he decided to make one out of leather. His leather bike saddles were a huge success, and the Brooks company still makes them in Birmingham, England, today.

The first leather saddles were more comfortable than the old wooden ones.

SPECIAL SADDLES

Some racers prefer lightweight leather saddles. To make them, a piece of thick leather is stretched across a light metal frame. Leather saddles usually become softer over time. Even lighter saddles are made of a strong, plastic material called **carbon fibre**, which is woven like fabric and then moulded into shape.

Racing saddles are designed for speed, not comfort.

Gears and brakes • Making the saddle

Putting it all together

The Finished Bike

The parts of a bike are made in many different places. Then they are all delivered to one factory, where they are put together to make the finished bike. The bikes go to a quality control department, where experts check that they have been put together correctly. They test each bike before it is put in a cardboard package and sent to the manufacturer's warehouse.

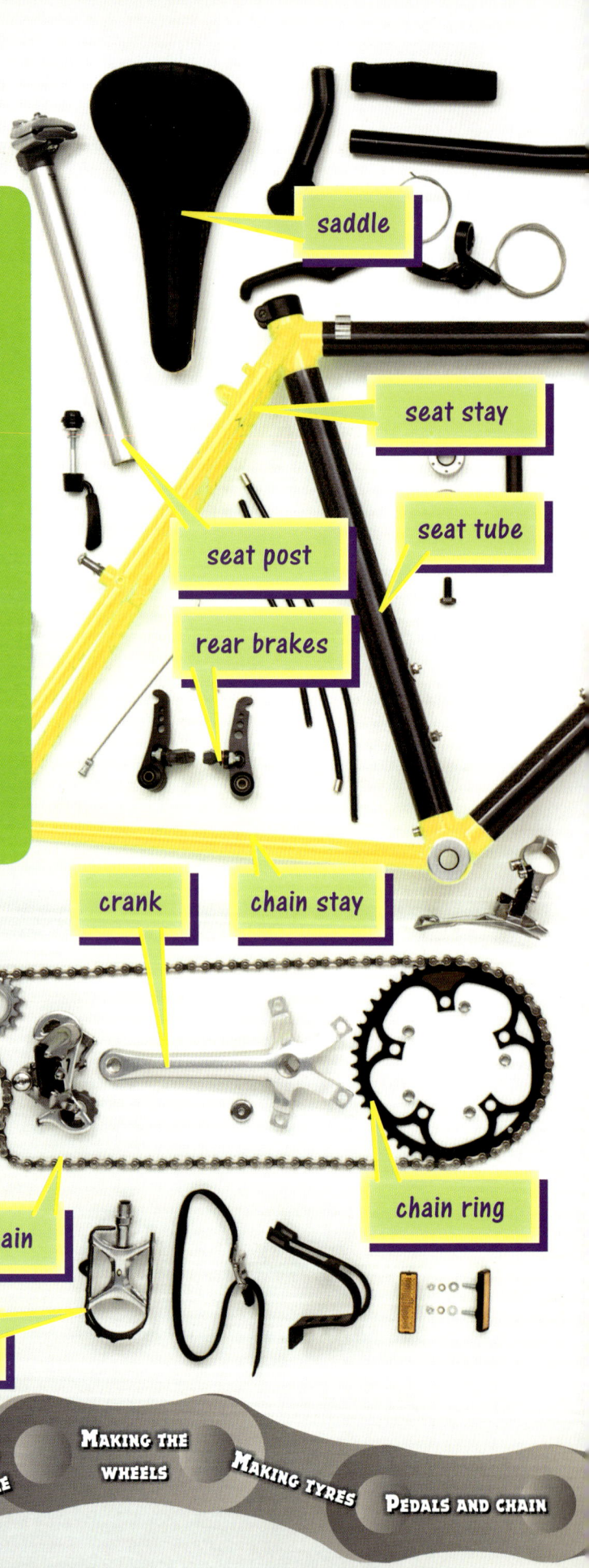

- saddle
- seat stay
- seat tube
- seat post
- rear brakes
- crank
- chain stay
- chain ring
- hub
- spoke
- sprockets
- chain
- pedal

Designing the bike · Making the frame · Painting the frame · Making the wheels · Making tyres · Pedals and chain

20

handlebars

⭐ MY JOB

Quality controller

"I work in quality control. It's my job to check each bike after it has been assembled. I make sure that all the parts have been put together correctly. I pay special attention to the brakes and check that the gears work properly. My company puts safety first and wants its customers to be happy with their new bike."

top tube

head tube

fork

down tube

front brakes

NAME THAT PART!

There are many parts to every bike. We have already met most of them in this book.

tyre

rim

valve

Gears and brakes

Making the saddle

Assembling the bike

21

Sports and races

There are many different cycling sports. Some bike races take place on a track inside a special stadium, called a velodrome. Others take place outdoors on the road. There are also off-road, cross-country races.

Olympic cycling

In the Olympic Games, there are nine different cycling events for men and nine for women. There are track races for individual riders and teams, road races, a mountain bike cross-country race, and a BMX event.

The Olympic velodrome track in London in 2012 was very fast and many riders set new world records.

Tour de France

The Tour de France is the most famous road race in the world. It was first held in 1903 and takes place every year. There are 21 stages, one a day, so the whole race takes 3 weeks. Each stage is timed, and the rider with the lowest time overall is the winner. The riders cover about 3 200 kilometres (1 990 miles) and the race finishes in Paris.

The race leader in the Tour de France wears a yellow jersey.

ROUGH RIDING

Mountain bikes have to be very sturdy, because the cross-country course is rough. BMX stands for 'bicycle motocross'. BMX races are usually on dirt tracks that go up and down hills, with lots of bumps and turns.

BIKING WORLD RECORDS

Fastest speeds
Men: 133 km/h (83 mph), Sam Whittingham (Canada)
Women: 121 km/h (75 mph), Barbara Buatois (France)

Track champions
Men: 250 m, 17.1 seconds, Rene Enders of Germany
Women: 500 m, 33.0 seconds, Anna Meares of Australia
Men: 1000 m, 58.9 seconds, Arnaud Tournant of France

BMX jumps off a ramp
Highest: 2.9 metres (9.5 feet), John Parker (USA)
Longest: 15.4 metres (50.5 feet), Mike Escamilla, USA

Some BMX riders do amazing stunts, including jumps, turns, twists and even somersaults.

To the bike shop

PACKED AND DELIVERED

The finished bikes are stored in the manufacturer's **warehouse**. When shops order bikes from the company, a lorry delivers the bikes. At the shop, the bikes are taken out of their packaging, checked again and then put on display. The bike-shop workers help customers to buy the right bike for their needs.

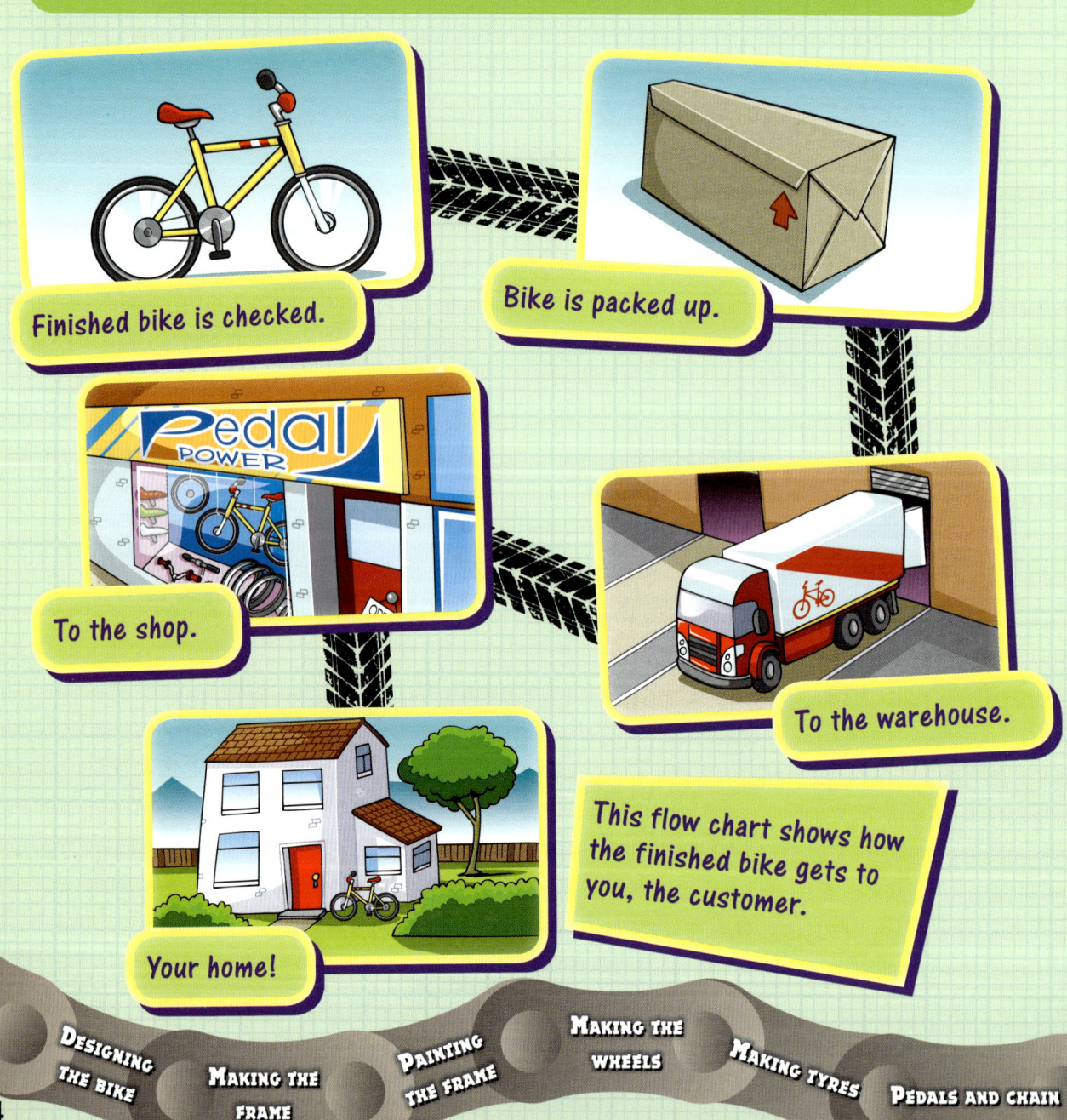

Finished bike is checked.

Bike is packed up.

To the shop.

To the warehouse.

This flow chart shows how the finished bike gets to you, the customer.

Your home!

Designing the bike · Making the frame · Painting the frame · Making the wheels · Making tyres · Pedals and chain

24

PARCELLING UP

Manufacturers turn the handlebars and sometimes leave off the pedals so that the bike fits into a flat pack of cardboard. In some cases they also take off the wheels and seat too. They wrap plastic and card around the parts to protect them. Some customers buy their bike online. When the bike arrives, they have to put the parts together.

Bikes are carefully packaged so that nothing gets damaged.

⭐ MY JOB

Bike mechanic

"I work in a bike shop. It's my job to unpack new bikes and make sure they are ready for customers to ride. I check all of the parts are attached properly, and I adjust the saddle and handlebars so that they are right for each cyclist. Customers also bring in bikes for me to adjust and repair."

Gears and brakes · Making the saddle · Assembling the bike · To the bike shop

Bits and pieces

See and be seen

In the bike shop you can buy lots of extras for your bike. Some of these are important for safety, such as lights and reflectors. A light means you can be seen by other traffic and it helps you to see the road ahead. A reflector is a piece of plastic that catches light from cars or other vehicles and throws it back towards them. This means that they see you and you are safer.

Try It!

There are lots of **accessories**, from bags and baskets to bottles and phone holders. Can you think up a new extra for your bike? Draw a diagram with labels to show how it might look.

Lights like these can be attached to any bike!

You will also need a bell to warn others that you are there, as well as a pump to fill your tyres with air. It's a good idea to buy a lock, to keep your bike secure when you leave it. Accessories are usually made by a wide range of different companies and are delivered to shops separately.

DID YOU KNOW?

Some bikes fold up so they can be carried around easily. The wheels fold around the frame and the saddle and handlebars can be lowered.

folded

unfolded

Safety first

HEADS UP

The most important item you need to go with your bike is a safety helmet. It is made of several different plastic materials. The inner part that fits onto your head is called a liner. It is made from plastic foam beads that are heated in a mould so they end up as one piece. The liner is then glued inside a harder plastic shell, or cover, which is also made in a mould. The cover is spray-painted.

Make sure your helmet is the right size and fits snugly.

The helmet has nylon straps to keep it secure on your head, and there are soft foam pads to make it comfortable.

Designing the bike · Making the frame · Painting the frame · Making the wheels · Making tyres · Pedals and chain

I CAN SEE YOU!

Bike shops also sell special clothing for cyclists. These items are usually made of a colourful reflective fabric, which means that other people on the roads can see cyclists easily. As well as jackets and vests, there are reflective arm and ankle bands.

Try It!

You can probably ride a bike very well, but do you know all the rules of the road? Ask at school about a cycle training programme. There are different levels, including for beginners. Learning to ride properly and safely can be fun.

It's important to learn the rules of the road.

Looking after your bike

If you look after your bike well, it will last longer and be safer to ride too. There are lots of things you can do yourself, but if you're not sure, always ask an adult for help and advice.

Check it over

Check the main parts of your bike regularly. First check that the brakes work properly. If you're not sure about them, take your bike to a bike repair shop. Then check your tyres. If there is any damage or too much wear, tell an adult. Here are some further tips:

✔ oil the chain regularly with bike **lube**

✔ check that the tyres are pumped up

✔ check that the handlebars are straight and tightly fixed.

It's important to check your bike before every ride.

KEEP IT CLEAN

You will need:
a bucket
soapy water (and clean water later)
rags and cloths
bike lube.

If your bike is muddy, wash it first with soapy water. Then use clean water to wash away the soap, which otherwise could cause rust. Dry it thoroughly with rags, and then polish it with a soft, clean cloth. Finally, oil the chain, and wipe off any extra oil.

TOOLKIT

Your bike might have come with a small toolkit. If not, ask an adult to help you get together a toolkit, with the following items.
- ✔ screwdrivers and spanners
- ✔ puncture repair kit, with rubber patches
- ✔ tyre levers, for taking off tyres and putting them back onto the rim.

Glossary

accessory extra part that goes with something larger

carbon fibre very strong, light material made of thin strands of carbon that are woven together and mixed with plastic

cassette collection of sprockets

design studio room where a designer plans the look of something

engineer person who builds machines

environmentally friendly good for the world around us

extruded pushed or squeezed out

lube short for *lubricant*, a special greasy oil that makes parts run smoothly

mould hollow container used to shape hot metal, plastic or food

nylon light, tough plastic thread

shifter lever that changes gears

sketch rough drawing

sprocket wheel with teeth around the edge that fit into the links of a chain

synthetic artificially made, not naturally produced

valve something that controls the flow of air or liquid

warehouse large building where goods are stored

welded joined together by heating and pressing

Index

accessories 26–27
BMX races 22, 23
brakes 17, 21, 30
buying a bike 24–27
chains 3, 14, 16, 30
designing a bike 4–5
first bikes 2–3
folding bikes 27
frames 6–7, 8, 27
gears 16–17, 21
handlebars 3, 17, 24, 27, 30
helmets 28
inner tubes 13
junior bikes 11
looking after your bike 30–31
materials 6, 7, 10, 12, 14, 17, 18, 19

mechanics 25
mountain bikes 3, 22, 23
number of bikes in the world 4
Olympic Games 22
paints, stickers and transfers 8–9
pedals 14, 15, 25
quality control 20, 21
saddles 18–19, 25, 27
safety 21, 26, 28–29, 30
tandems 15
toolkit 31
Tour de France 22
tyres and treads 10, 12–13, 30
wheels 2, 3, 10–11, 14, 25, 27
world records 23